SIEGFRIED

Driver-F
Drinks

The new dimension in
entertaining today

FOULSHAM BOOKS

FOREWORD

You don't have to use alcohol to mix exciting drinks in all sorts of flavours and colours. Leave it out, and you can still surprise your guests with stylish cocktail creations.

Shaking, stirring and decorating cocktails with no alcoholic ingredients is a trend which is catching on fast. People are starting to put as much care into creating drinks as they do into cooking. Whether your guests have to watch their alcohol intake because they're driving home, or for health or religious reasons, or because they want to have a good time and remember it the next day; there are plenty of reasons why non-alcoholic drinks are a good idea. You can mix a huge variety of lively cocktails and long drinks using fresh fruit juices and a few other ingredients. This book lets you into some of the secrets of having your own bar and offers plenty of recipe suggestions.

Cheers!

CONTENTS

TIPPLE
WITHOUT
TEARS

Mixing stylish drinks
that won't lose you
your driving licence is
a fast-growing trend.
Fruity or zesty
cocktails and long
drinks, colourfully
decorated, are a feast
for the eyes and the
palate. They may not
have any alcohol, but
they will still pleasantly
surprise your guests.

5

FRESH FRUIT & VEG

Most of these drinks are based on fruit and vegetable juices, and some on milk. Always use the freshest, highest-quality ingredients to give your drinks the most natural flavour you can. This is particularly important when you are mixing alcohol-free drinks, because you cannot disguise any shortcomings in the mixer by adding a shot of alcohol. If possible, squeeze your own fruit and vegetable juices. This is quick and easy to do for citrus fruits, but it is important not to squeeze the juice until just before you mix the drink. If you leave it standing for any length of time, it will start to lose its flavour. An electric juice-extractor will allow you to make your own delicious juices from a whole range of fresh fruits and vegetables. These include tomatoes, carrots, celery, beetroot, spinach, peas, fennel, parsley, cucumber, onion and endives.

Vegetable juices have a low calorie content, but are full of vitamins and minerals. To give these refreshing and unusual juices that little extra piquancy, try these combinations:

Tomato juice: Season with a little salt and pepper; fine on its own, or add chives, or onion or parsley juice.

Carrot juice: with celery, apple or lemon juice.

Celery juice: with avocado puree, apple or melon juice.

Beetroot juice: with orange, mango or melon juice.

Spinach juice: with peach or apple juice.

Fennel juice: with peach, cherry or rhubarb juice.

Pea juice: with grapefruit, melon or a little lemon juice.

Parsley juice: goes perfectly with any other type of juice.

Cucumber juice: with tomato, onion, carrot, or rhubarb juice, avocado puree or with chives.

Onion juice: with marrow, spinach, carrot or beetroot juice.

Endive juice: with pear, peach or apple juice.

If you want to sweeten your vegetable juice slightly, use honey or a little glucose. Of course, you won't always be able to make these juices yourself, and will have to use whatever is available in the shops, but many of these juices are commonly available. This alternative is best when you cannot get hold of fresh fruit of the right quality. When buying **fruit juice**, always go for those which contain 100% fruit and have no preservatives or other additives.

One exception to this is unsweetened pineapple

juice, in which a maximum of 3 grams of citric acid per litre is acceptable. Some fruit juices are made from concentrated fruit juice diluted with water, but they must be clearly labelled as having been made from concentrates. Sugar is sometimes added, but again it must be mentioned on the label.

Fruit nectars involve adding water to make them into fruit juice, or pulp or concentrates of these. As they are allowed to have up to 20% sugar added, they tend to contain more calories than fruit juices.

You will also find **fruit juice drinks** in your supermarket. These are drinks with a low fruit content (apple drinks and similar a minimum of 30%, citrus juices 6% and other drinks and mixtures a minimum of 10%). These fruit juice drinks are not recommended for mixing.

Although **"mixers"** like lemonade, bitter lemon, ginger ale and tonic water have a very low fruit content, they are ideal in combination with a variety of other drinks.

Syrups are also important ingredients for drinks and will give you interesting nuances of taste and colour. You can make sugar syrup yourself by mixing sugar and water in equal quantities and then boiling them. Skim off any foam from the top using a slotted spoon and leave the syrup to cool. If you bottle it and seal it well, it will keep for a while.

The other most common syrups are grenadine, made from pomegranates, peppermint, almond, lime, strawberry and coconut syrup. You may also be able to find very good syrups made from pineapple, bananas, mango, passion fruit and cranberries.

BE YOUR OWN BARTENDER

There are a number of practical aids you need in your own bar for mixing drinks and measuring the quantities of ingredients. Some of these you will already have amongst your kitchen equipment, but you will soon realise that purpose-made utensils will make life a great deal easier.

One important piece of equipment is a **cocktail shaker (1)**, which is used for shaking up ingredients which otherwise do not blend together very easily. If you only want to mix drinks in small quantities, then a traditional shaker is fine. It consists of three parts: a tumbler, a strainer and a lid. If you are having a cocktail party, you are better off with a Boston shaker. This is larger, consisting of a metal tumbler and a smaller glass one which fits neatly inside it. After it has been shaken, the drink is poured quickly through a strainer. However, a Boston shaker can be hard to find in shops.

The important thing when mixing drinks in a shaker is to do it quickly. Put the ice cubes into the tumbler and then add your prepared ingredients. Don't shake the drink for more than 10 to 20 seconds or the ice will start melting and water it down.

The **mixing jug (2)** holds a litre of liquid and has a spout. This is used to combine ingredients that mix easily and then pour them out before the ice starts melting. Instead of a mixing tumbler you can also use the glass tumbler part of a Boston shaker, or a glass carafe.

The **strainer (3)** is used to strain out ice cubes or lemon pips before you pour the drink into glasses.

The long handled **spoon (4)** is used for stirring and for measuring ingredients. It holds the equivalent of one teaspoon.

The **measuring beaker (5)** has a duel function, to measure out either 20 or 40 ml (1–2 fl. oz). This beaker is not expensive and can make life much easier.

Using an **ice bucket (6)** will prevent the ice from melting too quickly.

Ice cubes or crushed ice can be added to the drinks using the **tongs (7)** or the **scoop**.

Ingredients which are not already in a bottle with a spout should be transferred into a squeezy bottle or a **dash bottle (8)**.

The bar will also need a **lemon squeezer**, **fruit knife**, and a **chopping board**. A **corkscrew**, **champagne bottle top** and **fork** are also essential utensils.

Cocktail sticks and **colourful straws** are ideal for decorating drinks. **Stirrers** are available in many different styles and colours and

can also be used as decorations.

Many drinks are served with ice, and you can let your imagination run wild to add splashes of colour to your drinks. Make ice cubes with fruit juice, which will also prevent the drinks from becoming too watery. Alternatively, freeze fruit – together with stalks and leaves if you like – or mint leaves, inside the ice cube.

Choose the right glass for the right drink to give your cocktails the perfect touch. The glass should enhance the colour and aroma. Use one of the following glasses depending on the size of the cocktail:

Cocktail glasses (10), highball glasses (11), goblets (12), wine glasses (13), champagne glasses (14) and **sundae glasses (15)** for exotic drinks.

SPECIAL COOLERS TO SUIT EVERY TASTE

Fresh and colourful, sweet or savoury, these cocktails are the most versatile of all the alcohol-free drinks. Fruit and vegetables are at their best in these drinks, both as ingredients and decoration.

(Photo: Lucky Driver, Recipe page 12)

LUCKY DRIVER

Serves one

50 ml (1⅔ fl. oz) orange juice

50 ml (1⅔ fl. oz) grapefruit juice

50 ml (1⅔ fl. oz) pineapple juice

20 ml (⅔ fl. oz) lemon juice

20 ml (⅔ fl. oz) coconut cream

1 orange slice

1 lemon slice

Shake the fruit juices and coconut cream together with ice cubes in the cocktail shaker and then pour into a highball glass. Decorate with a slice of orange and a slice of lemon.

ORANGE LEMONADE

Serves one

50 ml (2 fl. oz) orange juice

20 ml (1 fl. oz) lemon juice

20 ml (1 fl. oz) sugar syrup

soda water

orange slices

Mix the fruit juices, syrup and ice cubes together in a tumbler, fill the glass with soda water and give it a quick stir. Serve with slices of orange and a straw.

STRAWBERRY PLANT

Serves one

2 large fresh strawberries

60 ml (2 fl. oz) orange juice

60 ml (2 fl. oz) pineapple juice

30 ml (1 fl. oz) lemon juice

30 ml (1 fl. oz) strawberry syrup

1 fresh strawberry

Blend the strawberries with the fruit juices and syrup in an electric mixer, then pour into a long glass. Decorate with a fresh strawberry.

REFRESHER

Serves one

50 ml (2 fl. oz) orange juice

20 ml (1 fl. oz) grenadine

soda water

orange slices

Put the orange juice and grenadine into a tumbler with ice cubes, then top up with soda water. Serve with slices of orange and a straw.

AMERICAN GLORY

Serves one

juice of ½ orange

2 dashes of sugar syrup

lemonade

orange slices

Put two ice cubes into a champagne glass and pour over the orange juice and syrup. Top up with lemonade and serve with slices of orange and a straw.

MISSISSIPPI

Serves one

80 ml (3 fl. oz) Ribena

80 ml (3 fl. oz) orange juice

orange slices

Put the Ribena, orange juice and ice cubes into a tumbler and give the mixture a quick stir. Add a straw and some orange slices and serve.

(Photo: clockwise from the top right hand side: Orange Lemonade, Mississippi, Strawberry Plant, Refresher, Lucky Driver, American Glory)

FRUIT CUP I

Serves one

80 ml (3 fl. oz) orange juice
60 ml (2 fl. oz) pineapple juice
40 ml (1⅓ fl. oz) lemon juice
20 ml (⅔ fl. oz) grenadine
1 orange slice
1 cocktail cherry

Mix the fruit juices, grenadine and ice cubes in the shaker and then pour into a highball glass. Decorate with the orange slice and cherry.

PRINCE IGOR

Serves one

40 ml (2 fl. oz) passion fruit juice
20 ml (1 fl. oz) lemon juice
20 ml (1 fl. oz) pineapple juice
bitter lemon
1 slice lemon
1 small sprig lemon balm

Pour the fruit juices into a tall glass and stir for a few minutes. Fill the glass up with bitter lemon and decorate the drink with a slice of lemon and the lemon balm.

(Photo: from left to right: Fruit Cup I, Prince Igor, Fruit Cup II, Driver)

FRUIT CUP II

Serves one

80 ml (3 fl. oz) passion fruit juice
40 ml (1½ fl. oz) pineapple juice
40 ml (1½ fl. oz) lemon juice
20 ml (⅔ fl. oz) orange juice
20 ml (⅔ fl. oz) grenadine
1 pineapple chunk
1 cocktail cherry
1 small sprig lemon balm

Mix the fruit juices, grenadine and ice cubes in the shaker and then pour into a tall glass. Decorate with pineapple, cherry and lemon balm.

DRIVER

Serves one

50 ml (2 fl. oz) passion fruit juice
40 ml (1½ fl. oz) peach juice
30 ml (1 fl. oz) coconut cream
20 ml (⅔ fl. oz) lemon juice
mineral water
1 slice kiwi fruit
1 cocktail cherry
1 small sprig mint

Put the fruit juices, coconut cream and ice into a tall glass. Stir and add top up with mineral water. Decorate with a slice of kiwi fruit, cherry and the sprig of mint.

GRAPEFRUIT HIGHBALL

Serves one

40 ml (2 fl. oz) grapefruit juice
20 ml (1 fl. oz) grenadine
soda water or ginger ale

Pour the grapefruit juice into a glass with the grenadine and stir them for a few moments before adding soda water or ginger ale.
(Photo: top left)

TROPICAL MAGIC

Serves one

40 ml (2 fl. oz) peach juice
40 ml (2 fl. oz) grapefruit juice
40 ml (2 fl. oz) banana purée
20 ml (1 fl. oz) grenadine
tonic water
1 slice peach

Mix the grenadine, fruit juices and ice together in the shaker before pouring into a tall glass. Top up with tonic water and decorate with a slice of peach.
(Photo: top middle)

BORNEO GOLD

Serves one

60 ml (3 fl. oz) apricot juice
40 ml (2 fl. oz) banana purée
20 ml (1 fl. oz) passion fruit juice
tonic water
½ banana

Put ice cubes in a tall glass and pour the fruit juice over them, before filling the glass with tonic water. Decorate with half a banana.
(Photo: top right)

JAVA DREAM

Serves one

40 ml (2 fl. oz) peach juice
40 ml (2 fl. oz) banana juice
40 ml (2 fl. oz) passion fruit juice
20 ml (1 fl. oz) grenadine
tonic water
1 slice peach
1 cocktail cherry

Shake the fruit juices, grenadine and ice together in the shaker, then pour into a tall glass. Fill the glass up with tonic water and decorate with a peach slice and cocktail cherry.
(Photo: below left)

AMBASSADOR

Serves one

60 ml (2 fl. oz) peach juice
60 ml (2 fl. oz) passion fruit juice
40 ml (1½ fl. oz) Roses lime juice
1 pineapple chunk
1 cocktail cherry
1 small sprig lemon balm

Pour the fruit juices into a tall glass and stir them. Decorate with pineapple and a cocktail cherry along with the lemon balm if you wish.
(Photo: below middle)

CORAL GLOW

Serves one

40 ml (1⅓ fl. oz) apricot juice
40 ml (1⅓ fl. oz) passion fruit juice
20 ml (⅔ fl. oz) cherry juice
20 ml (⅔ fl. oz) lemon juice
10 ml (⅓ fl. oz) grenadine
tonic water
2 cocktail cherries
1 slice lemon

Mix the fruit juices, grenadine and ice cubes in the shaker and then pour into a tall glass. Top up with tonic water and decorate with cherries and a slice of lemon before serving.
(Photo: below right)

Buccaneer Sunset

Serves one

40 ml (1⅓ fl. oz) apricot juice
40 ml (1⅓ fl. oz) pear juice
20 ml (⅔ fl. oz) cherry juice
20 ml (⅔ fl. oz) lemon juice
10 ml (⅓ fl. oz) grenadine
tonic water
1 whole lemon
1 cocktail cherry

Mix the juices together with the grenadine and ice cubes in the shaker. Pour the mixture into a tall glass and fill the glass with tonic water. Decorate with a twist of lemon rind and the cherry.

Peppermint Lemonade

Serves one

20 ml (1 fl. oz) peppermint syrup
20 ml (1 fl. oz) lemon juice
soda water

Put the syrup, lemon juice and ice cubes in a glass and top up with soda water. Serve simply with a straw.

SARATOGA COOLER

Serves one

20 ml 1 fl. oz)
grenadine

20 ml (1 fl. oz) lemon
juice

ginger ale

fruit

Put the grenadine and
lemon juice, together
with the ice cubes, into
a glass and add ginger
ale to fill the glass.
Decorate with fruit and
serve with a straw and
a cocktail spoon.

LEMON SQUASH

Serves one

Juice of ½ lemon

2 tsp. icing sugar

soda water

lemon slices

Put the lemon juice,
icing sugar and ice
cubes into a glass and
top up with soda water.
Add the lemon slices
and serve with a straw
and a cocktail spoon.
(Photo: left to right:
Peppermint Lemon-
ade, Buccaneer Sun-
set, Saratoga Cooler,
Lemon Squash)

LEMON COOLER

Serves one

3 tsp. sugar syrup
20 ml (1 fl. oz) lemon juice
ginger ale

Put the sugar syrup, lemon juice and ice cubes in a glass and add ginger ale.
(Photo: top left)

PEPPER TONIC

Serves one

20 ml (²/₃ fl. oz) lemon juice
30 ml (1 fl. oz) peppermint syrup
tonic water
1 whole lemon

Pour the lemon juice and peppermint syrup in a tall glass and add tonic water. Decorate with a twist of lemon rind.
(Photo: top middle)

GINGER COOLER

Serves one

50 ml (2 fl. oz) lemon juice
ginger ale

Half fill a glass with ice and pour in the lemon juice. Add ginger ale and serve decorated with a straw.
(Photo: top right)

PROOFLESS

Serves one

60 ml (2 fl. oz) freshly squeezed lime juice
40 ml (1⅓ fl. oz) Roses lime juice
tonic water
1 slice lime

Mix the fresh lime juice with the slightly sweeter Roses lime juice in a glass and then fill up the glass with tonic water. Decorate with a slice of lime.
(Photo: below left)

CHICAGO COOLER

Serves one

juice of ½ lemon
ginger ale
red grape juice

Half fill a tumbler with ice, then add the lemon juice and top up the glass with an equal mixture of ginger ale and red grape juice.
(Photo: below middle)

BRUNSWICK COOLER

Serves one

juice of ½ lemon
2 tsp. sugar syrup
ginger ale
fruit

Half fill a tumbler with ice, add the lemon juice and syrup. Top up with ginger ale, decorate with fruit and serve with a straw and cocktail spoon.
(Photo: below right)

AMERICAN LEMONADE

Serves one

juice of ½ lemon
2 dashes of sugar syrup
soda water
1 slice lemon

Half fill a sundae glass with ice and then add the lemon juice and sugar syrup. Top up with soda water and decorate with a slice of lemon and a straw.

BOSTON COOLER

Serves one

1 whole lemon
20 ml (⅔ fl. oz) grenadine
ginger ale

Put the grenadine and ice cubes together with a twist of lemon rind in a sundae glass. Then add the ginger ale and serve the drink with a straw.

PINEAPPLE SODA

Serves one

80 ml (3 fl. oz) pineapple juice

80 ml (3 fl. oz) soda water

pineapple chunks

Fill a glass with pineapple juice, soda water and two ice cubes. Decorate with the pineapple chunks.

BORA-BORA

Serves one

100 ml (3½ fl. oz) pineapple juice

60 ml (2 fl. oz) passion fruit juice

20 ml (⅔ fl. oz) lemon juice

10 ml (⅓ fl. oz) grenadine

1 pineapple ring

1 cocktail cherry

Mix the fruit juices, grenadine and ice cubes in the shaker before pouring into a glass. Decorate with the pineapple ring and cherry.
(Photo: from left to right: Boston Cooler, American Lemonade, Pineapple Soda, Bora-Bora)

23

BIRD OF PARADISE

Serves one

60 ml (2 fl. oz) pineapple juice

60 ml (2 fl. oz) passion fruit juice

60 ml (2 fl. oz) orange juice

10 ml (⅓ fl. oz) lemon juice

10 ml (⅓ fl. oz) grenadine

1 pineapple ring

1 cocktail cherry

Mix the fruit juices, grenadine and ice cubes in a shaker, then pour into a sundae glass. Decorate with a pineapple ring and cocktail cherry before serving.
(Photo: top right)

BLUE BATAVIA

Serves one

30 ml (1 fl. oz) pineapple juice

30 ml (1 fl. oz) pear juice

30 ml (1 fl. oz) passion fruit juice

30 ml (1 fl. oz) apricot juice

10 ml (⅓ fl. oz) lemon juice

10 ml (⅓ fl. oz) orange juice

bitter lemon

1 slice lemon

1 cocktail cherry

Mix the fruit juices together with the orange juice and ice in the shaker, then pour into a glass. Add the bitter lemon and decorate with a slice of lemon and a cocktail cherry.
(Photo: top middle)

BALI-BOO

Serves one

40 ml (2 fl. oz) pineapple juice

40 ml (2 fl. oz) passion fruit juice

40 ml (2 fl. oz) apricot juice

20 ml (1 fl. oz) orange syrup

bitter lemon

1 pineapple ring

1 cocktail cherry

Mix the fruit juices and ice together in the shaker. Pour into a glass and fill it up with bitter lemon. Decorate with a pineapple ring and cocktail cherry before serving.

MALAYIAN REFRESHER

Serves one

80 ml (3 fl. oz) pineapple juice

40 ml (1½ fl. oz) grapefruit juice

20 ml (¾ fl. oz) orange syrup

bitter lemon

1 pineapple ring

Mix the fruit juices, orange syrup and ice cubes in the mixing jug and then pour into a sundae glass. Fill the glass up with bitter lemon and decorate with a pineapple ring.
(Photo: below left)

PINEAPPLE COCKTAIL

Serves one

40 ml (1⅓ fl. oz) pineapple juice

30 ml (⅓ fl. oz) orange juice

pineapple chunks

Shake the fruit juices together with ice cubes in the shaker and then pour into a cocktail glass. Decorate with pineapple chunks.
(Photo: below middle)

PINEAPPLE POLL

Serves one

40 ml (2 fl. oz) pineapple syrup

juice of ½ lemon

soda water

pineapple chunks

Half fill a sundae glass with ice and then add the syrup and lemon juice. Top up with soda water and serve decorated with pineapple chunks, a cocktail spoon and a straw.
(Photo: below right)

BONGO

Serves one

70 ml (2⅓ fl. oz) pineapple juice
40 ml (1⅓ fl. oz) mango juice
40 ml (1⅓ fl. oz) lemon juice
30 ml (1 fl. oz) orange juice
20 ml (⅔ fl. oz) coconut cream
1 pineapple chunk
1 cocktail cherry
1 small sprig mint

Mix the fruit juices, coconut cream and ice cubes in the shaker and then pour into a tall glass. Decorate with a pineapple chunk, cherry and the mint.

QUEEN CHARLOTTE

Serves one

50 ml (2 fl. oz) almond milk
20 ml (1 fl. oz) raspberry juice
soda water

Put the almond milk and raspberry juice into a glass with some ice cubes and top up the drink with soda water. Serve with a straw.

(Photo: from left to right: Queen Charlotte, Bongo, Bicycle, Sunbreaker)

26

BICYCLE

Serves one

70 ml (2⅓ fl. oz) mango juice
40 ml (1⅓ fl. oz) lemon juice
20 ml (⅔ fl. oz) passion fruit juice
10 ml (⅓ fl. oz) grenadine
mineral water
1 pineapple chunk
1 cocktail cherry
1 small sprig lemon balm

Put the fruit juices and grenadine in a glass and stir before filling the glass up with mineral water. Decorate with the pineapple chunk, cherry and lemon balm.

SUNBREAKER

Serves one

80 ml (3 fl. oz) mango juice
20 ml (⅔ fl. oz) Roses lime juice
tonic water
1 slice orange
1 small sprig lemon balm

Pour the mango juice in a glass together with the Roses lime juice and top up with tonic water. Decorate with a slice of orange and the sprig of lemon balm.

SPLASH

Serves one

60 ml (2 fl. oz) mango
juice

30 ml (1 fl. oz) lemon
juice

30 ml (1 fl. oz) pineapple
juice

20 ml (⅔ fl. oz) almond
syrup

mineral water

1 pineapple chunk

1 cocktail cherry

1 small sprig lemon balm

Pour the fruit juices and almond syrup into a tall glass and stir, then add the mineral water. Before serving, decorate with the pineapple, cherry and lemon balm.
(Photo: Middle left)

ELDORADO

Serves one

40 ml (1⅓ fl. oz) guava
juice

40 ml 1⅓ fl. oz) orange
juice

40 ml 1⅓ fl. oz) passion
fruit juice

40 ml (1⅓ fl. oz)
pineapple juice

tonic water

1 pineapple ring

1 slice orange

1 cocktail cherry

Stir the fruit juices in the mixing jug with ice cubes and then pour into a tall glass. Add tonic water and decorate with the pineapple ring, orange slice and the cherry.
(Photo: background left)

BADEN-BADEN

Serves one

80 ml (3 fl. oz) morello
cherry juice

40 ml (1⅓ fl. oz) passion
fruit juice

30 ml (1 fl. oz) pineapple
juice

30 ml (1 fl. oz) Roses lime
juice

20 ml (⅔ fl. oz) lemon
juice

1 slice orange

1 cocktail cherry

1 small sprig lemon balm

Pour the fruit juices and lime juice over ice in a tall glass and stir for a few moments. Decorate with the orange slice, cherry and lemon balm.
(Photo: background right)

STEFFI-GRAF-COCKTAIL

Serves one

40 ml (1⅓ fl. oz) pear
juice

40 ml (1⅓ fl. oz) apricot
juice

40 ml (1⅓ fl. oz) kiwi fruit
juice

40 ml (1⅓ fl. oz) orange
juice

1 kiwi fruit slice

1 small cocktail pear

1 slice orange

Put the fruit juices in a cocktail glass and stir for a few moments. Spear the fruit on a cocktail stick and lay it over the glass.
(Photo: left)

CHERRY BLOSSOM

Serves one

60 ml (2 fl. oz) cherry
juice

40 ml (1⅓ fl. oz) orange
juice

40 ml (1⅓ fl. oz) apricot
juice

mineral water

1 cocktail cherry

1 slice lemon

Mix the fruit juices and ice in the shaker. Pour into a tall glass and serve with the cherry and orange slice.
(Photo: middle right)

POWER JUICE

Serves one

100 ml (4 fl. oz) beetroot
juice

100 ml (4 fl. oz) carrot
juice

20 ml (1 fl. oz) lemon
juice

pepper

1 long sliver of cucumber

Fill a tumbler with ice cubes and pour the vegetable juice over them. Sprinkle with a little pepper, give the mixture a quick stir and then decorate with the cucumber before serving.
(Photo: foreground right)

VIRGIN MARY

Serves one

200 ml (7 fl. oz) tomato juice

1 dash lemon juice

salt

pepper

Worcester sauce

tabasco

1 stick celery or radish

Mix all the juices together in the mixing jug and season to taste. Pour into a tall glass and add ice cubes and decorate with either a stick of celery or a piece of radish.
(Photo: top left)

TOMATO CRESS

Serves one

60 ml (3 fl. oz) tomato juice

20 ml (1 fl. oz) cream

Mix the tomato juice with the cream and some ice cubes in the mixing jug. Pour through a sieve into a cocktail glass. Decorate with cress and serve chilled.
(Photo: top middle)

TIP
Dry the cress and freeze it inside ice cubes.

CARLOTTA

Serves one

40 ml (1⅓ fl. oz) celery juice

40 ml (1⅓ fl. oz) carrot juice

40 ml (1⅓ fl. oz) apple juice

1 dash lemon juice

1 tsp. chopped parsley

Mix the juices, parsley and ice cubes in a mixing jug and then pour into a tall glass and serve.
(Photo: top right)

DUTCHMAN

Serves one

40 ml (1⅓ fl. oz) carrot juice

10 ml (⅓ fl. oz) white wine vinegar

30 ml (1 fl. oz) water

1 pinch curry powder

Shake the juice, curry powder and ice cubes vigorously in the cocktail shaker and then pour the drink into a chilled glass.
(Photo: below left)

COUNTRY DREAM

Serves one

50 ml (2 fl. oz) carrot juice

50 ml (2 fl. oz) apple juice

1 tsp. cream

Shake the juices and cream with ice in the shaker and pour immediately into a cocktail glass.
(Photo: below middle)

BAVARIAN TOMATO

Serves one

100 ml (4 fl. oz) tomato juice

25 ml (1 fl. oz) white wine vinegar

75 ml (3 fl. oz) water

1 tsp. caraway seeds

Mix all the ingredients together with ice cubes in the shaker and then pour into a tall glass.
(Photo: below right)

ICE-CREAM TEMPTATION

The vast range of flavours available provides a colourful mix to let your imagination run riot. Whether you prefer vanilla, pineapple or chocolate ice-cream, a talented bartender will always find the right drink to complement its taste. This is also true of the milk shakes which can be found at the end of the chapter.

(Photo: left Mint Ice-cream Soda, Aztec Fire, Recipes page 34)

AZTEC FIRE

Serves one

2 scoops vanilla
ice-cream

250 ml (½ pt) cold coffee

1 pinch cocoa powder

cinammon

Mix the ice-cream, coffee
and cocoa powder in a
mixing jug and then pour
into a tall glass. Sprinkle
with cinammon and
serve.

POLAR ORANGE

Serves one

2 scoops vanilla
ice-cream

40 ml (1⅔ fl. oz) milk

20 ml (⅔ fl. oz) orange
syrup

soda water

Put some ice in a glass
and then add the ice-
cream, milk and syrup.
Stir and add the soda
water. Serve simply with a
straw.

BLUE ICE

Serves one

2 scoops vanilla
ice-cream

20 ml (⅔ fl. oz) orange
juice

100 ml (4 fl. oz) milk

Mix all the ingredients
together with ice cubes in
a mixing jug, before pouring into a tall glass.

MINT ICE-CREAM SODA

Serves one

2 scoops vanilla
ice-cream

100 ml (4 fl. oz) milk

20 ml (⅔ fl. oz)
peppermint syrup

soda water

Put the ice-cream, milk
and syrup in a tall glass,
stir and then fill the glass
with soda water. Serve
with a straw and a cocktail
spoon.

CHOCOLATE MILKSHAKE

Serves one

2 scoops vanilla
ice-cream

50 ml (1⅔ fl. oz) milk

30 ml (1 fl. oz) chocolate
syrup

a little whipped cream

grated chocolate

Mix the ice-cream, milk
and syrup in the shaker,
pour into a tall glass and
top with whipped cream.
Sprinkle with chocolate
and serve immediately
with a straw.
*(Photo clockwise from
the top: Polar Orange,
Chocolate Milkshake,
Orange Shake, Mint Ice-
cream Soda, Aztec Fire,
Blue Ice)*

ORANGE SHAKE

Serves one

1 scoop vanilla ice-cream

100 ml (3 fl. oz) milk

80 ml (4 fl. oz) orange
juice

10 ml (⅔ fl. oz) cherry
syrup

1 tbsp. grated chocolate

1 tbsp. grated orange
rind

Mix the ice-cream, milk,
orange juice and syrup
together with some ice
cubes in the shaker and
then pour into a glass.
Sprinkle with chocolate
and orange rind before
serving.

SWEET SUSIE

Serves one

1 scoop vanilla ice-cream
1 scoop pineapple ice-cream
20 ml (⅔ fl. oz) raspberry juice
soda water
a little whipped cream
fresh strawberries

Put the ice-cream and raspberry juice in a glass and cover with soda water. Top with whipped cream and strawberries, then serve with a spoon and a straw.

BLACKBERRY FROST

Serves one

1 scoop vanilla ice-cream
30 ml (1 fl. oz) blackberry syrup
milk

Put the ice-cream and syrup in a glass and cover with chilled milk. Serve with a spoon and a straw.

Orange Ice-Cream Soda

Serves one

2 scoops vanilla
ice-cream

40 ml (1⅓ fl. oz) milk

20 ml (⅔ fl. oz) orange
juice

10 ml (⅓ fl. oz)
pineapple syrup

soda water

Put some ice cubes in
a tall glass and cover
with the ice-cream,
milk, orange juice and
syrup. Stir and then
add the soda water.
Serve with a straw.

Bilberry Glacier

Serves one

1 scoop vanilla
ice-cream

30 ml (1 fl. oz) bilberry
syrup

30 ml (1 fl. oz) milk

soda water

Mix the ice-cream,
syrup and milk in the
shaker with some ice
cubes. Pour into a tall
glass and serve with a
straw.
*(Photo: left to right:
Sweet Susie, Black-
berry Frost, Bilberry
Glacier, Blue Ice-
cream Soda)*

BANANA CREAM SODA

Serves one

2 scoops vanilla ice-cream

100 ml (4 fl. oz) banana purée

10 ml (⅓ fl. oz) lemon juice

soda water

Put the ice-cream and fruit juice in a long glass, stir and fill with soda water. Serve decorated with a straw and a cocktail spoon.
(Photo: top left)

COCA-COLA MALT MILK

Serves one

30 ml (1 fl. oz) chocolate syrup

50 ml (1⅔ fl. oz) cream

2 tsp. malted milk

Coca-Cola

Mix the chocolate syrup, cream, malted milk and ice cubes in the cocktail shaker. Pour into a glass, then add ice cold Coca-Cola and serve with a straw.
(Photo: top middle)

STRAWBERRY SODA

Serves one

1 scoop strawberry ice-cream

20 ml (⅔ fl. oz) lemon juice

20 ml (⅔ fl. oz) strawberry syrup

soda water

Shake the ice-cream, lemon juice, syrup and ice cubes in the cocktail shaker and then pour into a glass. Add the soda water and serve with a straw.
(Photo: top right)

ICE-CREAM SODA

Serves one

2 scoops ice-cream (any flavour)

soda water

Put the ice-cream in a glass and cover with soda water. Serve with a cocktail spoon and a straw.

MOCCA MIX

Serves 2

3 scoops chocolate ice-cream

1 tsp. mocca

250 ml (½ pt) milk

Mix all the ingredients in a mixing jug before pouring into a tall glass.
(Photo: below middle)

NIGHT CAP

Serves one

50 ml (1⅔ fl. oz) hot milk

20 ml (⅔ fl. oz) vanilla syrup

soda water

Put the milk in a glass with the syrup, stir for a few moments and then add soda water. Serve with a straw.
(Photo: below right)

ALMOND MILK

Serves one

160 ml (¼ pt) milk
40 ml (1⅓ fl. oz) almond syrup
1 dash grenadine
roasted flaked almonds

Shake the milk, almond syrup and grenadine together with some ice cubes in the cocktail shaker. Half fill a glass with ice cubes and pour the mixture over them. Decorate with flaked almonds and serve with a straw.
(Photo: background left)

TANGO

Serves one

60 ml (2 fl. oz) pineapple juice
60 ml (2 fl. oz) lemon juice
30 ml (1 fl. oz) coconut cream
30 ml (1 fl. oz) cream
10 ml (⅓ fl. oz) almond syrup
1 cocktail cherry

Mix the fruit juices, coconut cream, cream and syrup with ice cubes in the shaker and then pour into a tall glass. Decorate with a cocktail cherry.
(Photo: middle)

CARIBBEAN MILKSHAKE

Serves one

50 ml (1⅔ fl. oz) banana purée
50 ml (1⅔ fl. oz) pineapple juice
50 ml (1⅔ fl. oz) buttermilk
20 ml (⅔ fl. oz) orange juice
cinnamon

Mix all the ingredients in the cocktail shaker with some ice cubes and then pour into a glass and sprinkle with cinnamon.
(Photo: background)

FLORIDA MILK

Serves one

60 ml (2 fl. oz) milk
10 ml (⅓ fl. oz) orange juice
10 ml (⅓ fl. oz) lemon juice
10 ml (⅓ fl. oz) grenadine

Shake all the ingredients vigorously in the cocktail shaker. Pour into a cocktail glass.
(Photo: foreground left)

SUNDOWNER

Serves one

40 ml (1⅓ fl. oz) cream
20 ml (⅔ fl. oz) banana purée
10 ml (⅓ fl. oz) grenadine

Mix all the ingredients with ice cubes in the cocktail shaker and then pour into a cocktail glass.
(Photo: foreground)

TOMATO MILK

Serves one

40 ml (1⅓ fl. oz) tomato juice
juice ½ lemon
30 ml (1 fl. oz) milk
ground nutmeg

Mix all the ingredients in the cocktail shaker, pour into a glass and sprinkle with nutmeg.
(Photo: right)

ADD AN EGG

When egg mixes with fruit juice in the shaker, the result is a soft, creamy, tempting drink. Alternatively, let the egg yolk in the "Prairie Oyster" banish a hangover and remind you to stick to mixing alcohol-free drinks only!

(Photo: Boston Flip, Recipe page 44)

BOSTON FLIP

Serves one

30 ml (1 fl. oz) orange juice

10 ml (⅓ fl. oz) raspberry syrup

10 ml (⅓ fl. oz) peppermint syrup

1 egg

2 dashes lemon juice

soda water

ground nutmeg

Mix the fruit juices, syrups and egg in the cocktail shaker before pouring into a tall glass. Add soda water, sprinkle with nutmeg and serve with a straw.
(Photo: background left)

ORANGE CREAM FLIP

Serves one

30 ml (1 fl. oz) orange syrup

20 ml (⅔ fl. oz) raspberry juice

30 ml (1 fl. oz) cream

1 egg

soda water

pineapple chunks

Mix the orange syrup, fruit juice, cream and egg together with some ice cubes in the shaker. Pour into a champagne glass and top up with soda water. Decorate with pineapple chunks and serve with a cocktail spoon and a straw.
(Photo: background middle)

MANDARINE CREAM

Serves one

60 ml (2 fl. oz) orange juice

40 ml (1⅓ fl. oz) mandarine syrup

40 ml (1⅓ fl. oz) cream

1 dash grenadine

1 egg yolk

½ orange slice

1 cocktail cherry

Put the fruit juice, mandarine syrup, cream, grenadine, egg yolk and some ice cubes in the shaker and mix. Pour into a tall glass and decorate with the orange slice and cherry.
(Photo: middle)

EXPULSION

Serves one

20 ml (⅔ fl. oz) orange juice

2 egg yolks

1 tsp. sugar

hot water

Mix the juice, egg yolks and sugar in a mixing jug. Pour into a glass and add hot water.
(Photo: foreground left)

SPORTSMAN

Serves one

40 ml (1⅓ fl. oz) orange juice

20 ml (⅔ fl. oz) lemon juice

20 ml (⅔ fl. oz) grenadine

1 egg yolk

1 slice orange

Mix all the ingredients together in the shaker and pour into a tumbler. Decorate with a slice of orange.
(Photo: foreground)

ORANGE EGG NOG

Serves one

40 ml (1⅓ fl. oz) orange syrup

20 ml (⅔ fl. oz) cream

20 ml (⅔ fl. oz) milk

1 egg

Mix all ingredients in the shaker and pour into a champagne glass. Serve with a straw.
(Photo: right)

SPORTS FLIP

Serves one

60 ml (2 fl. oz) orange juice
30 ml (1 fl. oz) lemon juice
30 ml (1 fl. oz) passion fruit juice
10 ml (⅓ fl. oz) banana syrup
10 ml (⅓ fl. oz) grenadine
1 egg yolk

Mix all the ingredients thoroughly together with ice cubes in the shaker and pour the mixture into a tall glass.

BREAKFAST DRINK

Serves one

60 ml (2 fl. oz) orange juice
10 ml (⅓ fl. oz) grenadine
1 tsp. egg white

Mix all the ingredients with ice cubes in the shaker before pouring into a cocktail glass.

OFFENBURG FLIP

Serves one

40 ml (1 ⅓ fl. oz) orange juice
40 ml (1 ⅓ fl. oz) banana syrup
20 ml (⅔ fl. oz) lemon juice
1 egg yolk
½ banana

Put all the ingredients into an electric mixer and liquidise. Pour into a tall glass.

EGG LEMONADE

Serves one

10 ml (⅓ fl. oz) lemon juice
10 ml (⅓ fl. oz) sugar syrup
1 egg
20 ml (⅔ fl. oz) water

Mix all the ingredients together in the shaker and them pour into a glass.
(Photo: left to right: Breakfast Drink, Sports Flip, Offenburg Flip, Egg Lemonade)

GOLDEN FIZZ

Serves one

40 ml (1⅓ fl. oz) lemon juice

10 ml (⅓ fl. oz) ginger syrup

1 egg yolk

soda water

icing sugar

Shake the lemon juice, syrup and egg yolk with ice cubes in the shaker, and then pour into a glass. Add soda water, sprinkle with icing sugar and serve with a straw.
(Photo: left)

ATHLETIC

Serves one

60 ml (2 fl. oz) grape juice

60 ml (2 fl. oz) cream

20 ml (⅔ fl. oz) lemon juice

1 tsp. sugar

1 egg yolk

soda water

Shake the fruit juice, cream, sugar and egg yolk vigorously in the shaker and then pour into a glass. Add soda water.

EGG ICE-CREAM FLIP

Serves one

1 scoop vanilla ice-cream

20 ml (⅔ fl. oz) vanilla syrup

1 egg

soda water

1 cocktail cherry

Mix the ice-cream, syrup and egg together in the shaker and then pour into a glass. Top up with soda and decorate with the cherry and a straw before serving.
(Photo: top right)

GLASGOW FLIP

Serves one

20 ml (⅔ fl. oz) lemon juice

20 ml (⅔ fl. oz) sugar syrup

1 egg

ginger ale

Pour the lemon juice, syrup, and egg into a glass with some ice cubes, stir for a few moments and add the ginger ale. Serve with a straw.
(Photo: below left)

GRAPE EGG NOG

Serves one

80 ml (3 fl. oz) red grape juice

80 ml (3 fl. oz) milk

10 ml (⅓ fl. oz) sugar syrup

1 egg yolk

Mix all the ingredients in the shaker and then pour into a tall glass.

Variation
You can also prepare this drink using blackcurrant, thus creating a new Egg Nog.
(Photo: Below middle)

CANAAN

Serves one

150 ml (¼ pt) milk

1 egg

2 tsp. honey

cinnamon

Stir the milk, egg and honey in the mixing jug together with some ice cubes. Pour into a tall glass and sprinkle with cinnamon.

GINGER ALE FLIP

Serves one

3 tsp. sugar syrup
1 egg yolk
ginger ale

Mix the syrup and egg yolk in the shaker with some ice cubes and then pour into a champagne glass. Top up with chilled ginger ale.

JOGGING

Serves one

1 scoop chocolate ice-cream
100 ml (3½ fl. oz) milk
1 egg yolk
1 dash lemon juice
1 tsp. sugar
grated chocolate

Stir the ice-cream together with the milk, egg yolk, lemon juice and sugar in the mixing jug. Pour into a tall glass and sprinkle with grated chocolate before serving.

COFFEE FLIP

Serves one

40 ml (1 fl. oz) coffee
1 tsp. sugar syrup
1 egg
ground nutmeg

Mix the coffee, syrup and egg in the shaker with some ice, and then pour the mixture into a glass. Sprinkle with nutmeg and serve.

FLIP + FLAP

Serves one

200 ml (7 fl. oz) milk
2 tsp. chocolate syrup
1 egg yolk
1 tsp. instant coffee
chocolate slivers

Whip up the milk, syrup, egg yolk and coffee with ice cubes in an electric mixer. Pour into a tall glass and decorate with slivers of chocolate.
(Photo: from left to right: Jogging, Ginger Ale Flip, Flip + Flap, Coffee Flip)

"Skin Deep"

Serves one

30 ml (1 fl. oz) raspberry juice

1 egg

milk

Shake the juice and egg up in the shaker and pour into a glass. Add ice cold milk.

Sanddorn Flip

Serves one

200 ml (7 fl. oz) milk

20 ml (⅔ fl. oz) grenadine

1 egg yolk

Mix well all the ingredients with ice in the shaker and then pour into an extra long glass.

Honey Flip

Serves one

200 ml (7 fl. oz) milk

20 ml (⅔ fl. oz) blackcurrant juice

10 ml (⅓ fl. oz) honey

1 egg yolk

Mix all the ingredients thoroughly in the shaker and then pour into an extra long glass.

Blackforest Flip

Serves one

60 ml (2 fl. oz) Morello cherry juice

20 ml (⅔ fl. oz) Roses lime juice

10 ml (⅓ fl. oz) lemon juice

1 egg yolk

1 small sprig lemon balm

Mix the fruit juices, lime juice in the shaker with the egg and some ice cubes. Pour into a long glass and decorate with a sprig of lemon balm.

Pineapple Flip

Serves one

30 ml (1 fl. oz) pineapple juice

20 ml (⅔ fl. oz) orange juice

1 egg yolk

soda water

Mix the fruit juices and egg yolk in the shaker with some ice cubes and then pour into a glass. Add the soda water and serve.

Prairie Oyster

Serves one

2 tbsp. tomato sauce

3 dashes Worcester sauce

2 dashes lemon juice

salt

1 egg yolk

pepper

paprika

tabasco

Put the ketchup, Worcester sauce, lemon juice and a pinch of salt into a shallow glass and stir. Add the egg yolk and season to taste.

(Photo: clockwise from top right: Honey Flip, Prairie Oyster, Pineapple Flip, Blackforest Flip, Skin Deep, Sanddorn Flip)

THE COCKTAIL PARTY

Although punches have been with us for a long time, they are still so popular that people are always on the look-out for new combination ideas.

They can also be a lot of fun for children's parties, where the children can decorate the drinks themselves.

(Photo: Fruit Salad Punch, recipe page 56)

FRUIT SALAD PUNCH

Serves 5–10

2 tart apples
1 pear
1 banana
1 orange
500 ml (1 pt) orange juice
500 ml (1 pt) apple juice
200 ml (½ pt) banana purée
100 ml (¼ pt) pear juice
300 ml (¾ pt) soda water

Wash the apples and pears, cut them in half and slice thinly. Peel the banana and orange, cut into slices and then quarter the orange slices once more. Put the fruit with the juice into a punch bowl and chill. Then add the soda water and serve.
(Photo: top left)

LEMON PUNCH

Serves 5–10

2 whole lemons
1 whole orange
500 ml (1 pt) pineapple juice
20 cl (½ pt) orange juice
10 cl (¼ pt) lemon juice
10 cl (¼ pt) sugar syrup
½ l (1 pt) bitter lemon
40 cl (¾ pt) soda water

Peel the lemons and the orange and cut into slices. Quarter slices and put them into the punch bowl with the rind, fruit juice and syrup. Stir and chill the mixture. Before serving, remove the rind and add ice cubes, bitter lemon and soda.
(Photo: top middle)

MALAYAN PUNCH

Serves 10–15

4 l (7 pt) pineapple juice
1 l (2 pt) grapefruit juice
250 ml (½ pt) orange juice
bitter lemon
pineapple rings

Mix the fruit juice in a punch bowl and set aside to chill. Fill each glass two-thirds full of punch and then top up with bitter lemon. Decorate the glasses with pineapple rings.
(Photo: top right)

GOLDEN PUNCH

Serves 10–15

2 l (4 pt) banana juice
2 l (4 pt) apricot juice
1 l (2 pt) passion fruit juice
tonic water
bananas

Mix the fruit juice in a punch bowl, then set aside to chill. Fill each glass two thirds full of punch and then top up with tonic water. Decorate each glass with half a banana.
(Photo: below)

FRUIT CUP

Serves 10–15

2 l (4 pt) orange juice
2 l (4 pt) pineapple juice
¼ l (½ pt) lemon juice
¼ l (½ pt) grenadine
1 tin lychees
1 tin papayas
7 kiwi fruits, sliced
tonic water

Put the fruit juices with the grenadine in a punch bowl. Drain the tinned fruit and add to mixture together with the kiwi fruit. Chill the punch and then fill each glass two-thirds full, add fruit and top up with tonic water.
(Photo: left)

PINEAPPLE PUNCH

Serves 5–10 people

1 fresh pineapple
100 ml (¼ pt) pineapple syrup
100 ml (¼ pt) lemon juice
1 l (2 pt) ginger ale
400 ml (¾ pt) soda water

Slice the pineapple, remove the stalk, peel the slices, cut them into eight and then put them in the punch bowl with the fruit juice. Chill the mixture and then add the ginger ale and soda water.
(Photo: front right)

PIRATE PUNCH

Serves 10–15

2 l (4 pt) apricot juice
2 l (4 pt) pear juice
500 ml (1 pt) cherry juice
250 ml (½ pt) lemon juice
250 ml (½ pt) grenadine
tonic water
whole lemons
cocktail cherries

Put the fruit juices and grenadine in the punch bowl, stir and set aside to chill. Fill glasses two-thirds full with punch and top up with tonic water. Decorate each glass with a spiral of lemon rind and a cherry.
(Photo: middle)

TIP

Make ice cubes with the same fruit juice as that used in your punch, and this will help to keep the punch cool and avoid watering it down as happens with normal ice cubes. Apricot-coloured and cherry-coloured ice cubes are also attractive decorative touches.

BATAVIA PUNCH

Serves 10–15

2 l (4 pt) pineapple juice
1 l (2 pt) pear juice
1 l (2 pt) passion fruit juice
1 l (2 pt) apricot juice
50 ml (2 fl. oz) lemon juice
100 ml (¼ pt) orange juice
bitter lemon
lemon slices
cocktail cherries

Put the fruit juices into a punch bowl, stir and chill. Fill each glass two-thirds full with punch and top up with bitter lemon. Decorate each glass with a slice of lemon and a cocktail cherry.
(Photo: left)

BERRY PUNCH

Serves 5–10

100 g (4 oz) raspberries
100 g (4 oz) strawberries
100 g (4 oz) blackberries
100 ml (¼ pt) raspberry syrup
100 ml (¼ pt) strawberry syrup
100 ml (¼ pt) lemon juice
1 l (2 pt) blackberry juice
40 ml (¾ pt) soda water

Wash the fruit, cut in half and put into the bowl with the syrup and fruit juices. Stir and chill. Add ice cubes and soda water before serving.
(Photo: foreground)

MELON PUNCH

Serves 5–10

1 water-melon
1 honeydew melon
150 ml (¼ pt) mandarine syrup
70 ml (2 fl. oz) lime syrup
2 l (4 pt) lemonade

Cut honeydew melon in half, remove the pips with a spoon and remove the flesh with a melon scoop. Then slice the top off the water-melon and do the same. Put 4 scoops of honey and water melon balls per person into the hollowed out water-melon, fill with mandarine and lime syrup and top up with lemonade. Stir the punch and serve fresh. It is best to serve the melon on a plate or in a bowl lined with a serviette.
(Photo: back left)

CORAL PUNCH

Serves 10–15

2 l (4 pt) apricot juice
2 l (4 pt) passion fruit juice
½ l (1 pt) cherry juice
¼ l (½ pt) grenadine
tonic water
cocktail cherries
lemon slices

Put the fruit juices and grenadine in the bowl, stir and chill. Fill each glass two-thirds full with punch and top up with tonic water. Decorate each glass with a cocktail cherry and a slice of lemon.
(Photo: right)

Banana Punch

Serves 5–10

5 bananas
2 kiwi fruits
700 ml (1¼ pt) banana purée
100 ml (¼ pt) orange juice
100 ml (¼ pt) lemon juice
100 ml (¼ pt) pineapple juice
500 ml (1 pt) soda water

Peel the bananas and kiwi fruits and cut into small pieces. Put the fruit pieces and juice into a bowl, stir and chill. Add ice cubes and soda water before serving.

TIP

Mix the banana slices with lemon juice to prevent them from turning brown.

GRAPE PUNCH

Serves 5–10

100 g (4 oz) black grapes

100 g (4 oz) white grapes

500 ml (1 pt) black grape juice

500 ml (1 pt) white grape juice

100 ml (¼ pt) lemon juice

500 ml (1 pt) soda water

Wash the grapes carefully in warm water, cut in half and remove the pips. Put the fruit and fruit juice in the bowl, stir and chill. Add soda water and serve.
(Photo: top right)

KIWI PUNCH

Serves 5–10

6 kiwi fruits

80 ml (3 fl. oz) lemon juice

30 ml (1 fl. oz) sugar syrup

1 l (2 pt) ginger ale

400 ml (¾ pt) soda water

Peel and slice the kiwi fruits, then put into a bowl. Add the salt and syrup and leave for an hour to chill. Fill the bowl with ginger ale and soda water before serving.
(Photo: below right)

W. Foulsham & Co. Ltd.
London · New York · Toronto · Cape Town · Sydney

W. Foulsham & Company Limited
Yeovil Road, Slough, Berkshire, SL1 4JH

ISBN 0-572-01519-4
Originally published by Falken Verlag GmbH, 6722
Niedernhausen, West Germany. This English language edition
Copyright © 1989 W. Foulsham & Co. Ltd.
All rights reserved.

Photoset by Rowland Phototypesetting Limited, Bury St Edmunds, Suffolk
Printed in Hong Kong